I AM MOTIVATION

I AM SUCCESS

Inspirational Quotes to Unleash Your Greatness

Kendell Myers

ISBN: 978-0-578-95148-5

First Printing Edition, 2021

FOREWORD
BY REGELINE "Gigi" SABBAT

The Author Kendell Myers takes us on a journey, in which he explains how people can overcome their personal challenges of life, similar to how he overcame his own personal challenges. Author Kendell Myers's testimony is one of strength, courage, and hope. This book is truly a survivor's guide to overcoming personal challenges in your life.

This book includes over 100 empowering quotes by Author Kendell Myers that provide inspiration that will help you unleash your inherent greatness.

This book is a must read.

From the Author

I wanted to write a motivational book for a long time because I always had inspiring thoughts that I would give to my family, friends, and even myself. Even though this was a desire, I never made the time to do so until I faced an unexpected setback. I was drowning in depression. I felt overly stressed and defeated, but writing my amazing quotes was the lifeline that caused me to float until I could swim back to the shore of life. My own words caused me to thrive in this dark place.

My book is for:

The **motivators.**

Those who **need** motivation.

Those who are **trying** to get over the past.

Those who are trying to **overcome** challenging obstacles.

I hope you feel the passion behind every one of my words as I did.

Wear your crown high kings and queens.

Kendell Myers

"

Never consider yourself
last just because someone
started before you. You
have your **OWN** race to
run.

"

MISTAKES are a part of life and they will happen more than once. There are lessons to be learned, and it takes a growing person (you) to recognize that.

"

You have a great
GIFT inside you.
It takes for you to
know and the
world to find out.

"

3

Yes, **SETBACKS** hurt. But you know what hurts more? When you don't continue what you started.

Everyone will not **BELIEVE** in your cause. That doesn't mean your cause finishes there.

"There are two l's you you can take – a loss or a lesson. It's your **CHOICE** of which one you choose."

LET your positive waterfall drown the negative fish in the sea.

"

The invisible chain
that's dragging you
down can be **BROKEN**
at any time.

"

8

"

Your **TEMPLE** is
your kingdom. Treat
it like royalty or it will
be destroyed.

"

Success is for everyone, but to know that, you must not **QUIT**.

If you mean it, believe it.

If you say it, do it.

If you go for it, put
100 percent into it.

Be **GRATEFUL** for the small things you have, because someone wishes for it every day.

God has a **PLAN** for
you. Let His vision
lead you to happiness.

"

We all have been hurt
before, even successful
people. You don't hear
them making that an
EXCUSE.

"

Change your middle name to **GREATNESS** because it's inside of you.

Your favorite millionaire walks the same streets as you do – one **FOOT** at a time.

You **CLIMB** that mountain even if it takes your hands and feet.

"

This is not a sprint.
It's a marathon. The
JOURNEY is longer,
but treasures of a
lifetime are at the
finish line.

"

Don't miss out on your blessing being stuck on what's **HOLDING** you back.

Everyone has a **PAST**.
That doesn't mean it
should effect your future.

The more you continue to **GROW**, you will realize every day how far you came.

"

Don't read too far into anyone's success. You are writing **YOUR** book. Keep your eyes on that.

"

The tunnel might seem dark now, but there is a **LIGHT** at the end. Keep going with full steam.

You came too **FAR** to give up now. What don't kill you makes you stronger.

You were born to
be great. Now your
FUTURE is waiting on
you to showcase it.

Life is like an eagle.

The higher you **SOAR**,

the more you see.

Show people who you really are and you will always be **RESPECTED**.

Nothing is wrong with not having it all figured out now. It's a **PROCESS**. Everything takes time and patience.

This is not court. No jury has **CONTROL** over your verdict.

"

You are **FREE** to do whatever you want. Just make sure it makes you happy to do it.

"

Whenever you feel stressed, take a step back and **PACE** yourself. Don't try to take on the whole world all at once.

Step by Step

"

You will fail.

Don't let that **DEFEAT**

your Dream.

"

The sweetest revenge is **CONQUERING** your success that no one saw coming.

"

Some of the most
beautiful trees grow
in the **WILDERNESS**.

"

"

Don't be afraid to be **ALONE**. You think the best when you have no distraction.

"

"

You are the commander
in chief of your head.
Let it lead your **MIND** in
the right direction.

"

If you still have the same **MINDSET** after 365 days, you haven't tried enough new things.

"

No one will help you
come in first place. That
TAKES your blood, sweat,
and tears.

"

Learning how to **SACRIFICE** will allow you to achieve your dreams.

39

It's easy to say *no*. Say
YES to yourself first
not them.

DREAMS never stop.

Only you do.

Don't be **AFRAID** to step outside the box. You never know what your true talents will be.

As long as you are being **PRODUCTIVE** toward your goals, don't beat yourself up. You are doing a good job, and you will be there soon.

"

God makes no mistakes.
It happened for a
REASON. Take heed to
the lesson.

"

"Self is a strong word that goes in front of everything you stand for. Find self, and you will find **FREEDOM**."

FAITH is that life vest that keeps you safe when your ship is going down.

Allow faith to **LEAD** you to your destiny when it is hard for your eyes to see the finish line.

"

Just because they have
the same shoe size as
you, does not mean your
FOOTPRINT match.

"

We all know what to do to solve our problems. Some of us are too afraid to go with the **SOLUTION**.

Be **REAL** with yourself
and go with what's
best for you.

Most doors close for a **REASON**. Don't stay their trying to figure out why. Embrace your new ones.

Strong will is when you are **HUNGRY** and success is the only thing to fill you up.

Be four steps **AHEAD**.
Stay ready so you don't
have to get ready.

"During the race, obstacles come in all shapes and sizes. Faith **HELPS** you start and finish the race."

Stay **DEDICATED** to your future. You are up next.

"

Wisdom come from past
mistakes and lessons
that you **GROW** from.

"

A building is never
instantly made. It
takes brick by brick to
complete the structure.
That's the journey of
LIFE.

Use your **FAILURES** to learn. There is always a way out of no way.

If you are **PASSIONATE**
about it, do it.

Body language tells a **STORY** about how passionate you are about it.

Work ethic will out
class **BRILLANCE**
any day.

Say these four words out loud. **I AM A WINNER**. Simple but powerful. Now repeat every day.

Whatever you are going
through today will not
LAST forever.

"

Uncomfortable positions
make the greatest
CHAMPIONS.

"

Life is full of **BLESSINGS**.

Let God work His magic.

You **DESERVE** the best.

You work too hard for it.

Energy is **DETERMINED** by the things and the people you keep around.

"

Even when you are down,
your **SMILE** will keep you
up.

"

You will look back at a day like this and say, wow, I came **FAR**.

Grind harder than yesterday and see how **SUCCESSFUL** you can become.

Whatever you do, be **CONFIDENT** doing it.

"

BRANDING yourself will make a better life towards your future.

"

Staring in your rear view will only cause you to **MISS** your next exit, where your GPS is leading you.

The number one support
you need is **YOURSELF**.

Learn how to **ADAPT** when things don't go your way. You will know how to handle it better.

> You have all the keys you
> need. You just need to
> learn how to **UNLOCK**
> the doors.

Try it before anybody
TELL you not to try it.

Believe in yourself.
The only way is **UP**
from here.

TROUBLES comes and goes.

When dedicated, no **OBSTACLES** will stop you.

The more you grow your **STRENGTHS**, you will have no weaknesses.

God made you.
NOTHING or no one
can tear you down.

"

As long as you have faith in your plan and God by your side, you can **CONQUER** the world.

"

The only person you are **COMPETING** with is yourself. You definitely don't want to lose to that person.

That question we have about bettering our lives, the **ANSWER** is inside of us. You have to fight for it.

Turn that PAIN
into **POWER**.

Keep **PUSHING**

towards greatness.

You will **SAVE** someone's life one day with your goals and dreams.

Stay **AWARE**. Your blessing is coming.

"

It's simple. Work **HARD** now to play hard later.

"

BUILD towards your purpose every day.

Always have an ACE up your sleeve. **NEVER** show your whole hand at once.

Pursuit of happiness starts
with three letters- **Y.O.U**.

A **TRUE** champion is
built from the ground
up.

CREATE the space to have focus and faith.

"

ARTISTS are not just someone with a paintbrush or a mic. They also create visions that tell the story of the past, present, and future.

"

If you keep practicing your skills, you will become **GREATER** than you ever imagined.

POSITIVE energy defends
the odds against you.

The more you speak your

dreams into **EXISTENCE**,

It will become your reality.

"

Make a new **COMMITMENT** to yourself each and every day. Keep your eyes on it.

"

All **PROGRESS** is a good
thing even if it's small.
It all means you are
MOVING FORWARD.

Life has no **BOUNDARIES**.
Allow your mind to see
clearly so you can enjoy
life.

WARRIORS are made to be different sizes with different skills, mindsets, and duties. That is all of us.

"

Time will only tell how successful you will become. Be **PATIENCE** and pace yourself. The best things takes time.

"

Kings and Queens have down days. You don't see them changing their **TITLES**.

If your faith is not
BROKEN, nothing is.

When **PRESSURE** is forced down, it builds enough to shoot up. Stay down until the come-up.

CIRCUMSTANCES
cause frustrations, but
you will be more frustrated
if you allow the
circumstances to kill your
dreams.

"

They are laughing in your face now. **WAIT** until they see your success. Their face will look completely different then.

"

A life of hard work will
create success for your
family and your **FUTURE**.

"

You will always be on a road less traveled. That means you are on the right **PATH**.

"
Gold and money are not the only thing worth a lot. People with abnormal ambition that reach their **HIGHEST** peak are worth more.
"

The road to greatness have already been paved. **WALK** down it with faith, confidence, and dedication.

"

The purpose of life is to **FULFILL** destiny by fighting for your deepest passions even when it requires more energy than you thought.

"

Every superhero doesn't wear a mask and a cape. Just look in the **MIRROR** and go save the world.

"It's not about how long it takes to get to the finish line. It's about the **ACCOMPLISHMENT** of crossing it."

Without walking through **DIFFICULT** trials, we cannot help ourselves nor others.

Keep your inner **FLAME**
burning bright.

The world is very big.
It's still a lot more to
FIND out about yourself.

"

Nothing's wrong with putting **YOURSELF** first. If you don't, you will always finish last.

"

"

Change is powerful.
It will drive you to
conquer the
UNBELIEVABLE.

"

When you are pursuing your passions, don't worry about money. Everything will **FOLLOW**.

LIFE DON'T GET NO EASIER, YOU ONLY GET STRONGER.

Made in the USA
Coppell, TX
28 September 2021